HOW TO FIND A TEACHING JOB
A Guide for Success

Genny Cramer and Beth Hurst
Southwest Missouri State University

Merrill,
an imprint of Prentice Hall
Upper Saddle River, New Jersey   *Columbus, Ohio*

1

Editor: Debra A. Stollenwerk
Production Editor: JoEllen Gohr
Cover Designer: Diane C. Lorenzo
Cover Art: © Photodisk, Inc.
Production Manager: Pamela Bennett
Director of Marketing: Kevin Flanagan
Marketing Manager: Suzanne Stanton
Marketing Coordinator: Krista Groshong

Printed in the United States of America

10 9 8 7 6 5 4 3 2 1

ISBN: 0-13-013605-0

DEDICATION

*T*o my accepting and encouraging colleague, Beth Hurst; to my cherished husband and editor, Carter Cramer; and to my beloved daughters and friends, Stephanie and Megan Cramer. GC

*T*o my writing teachers: Genny Cramer, Ginny Reding, Aunt Mary, and my dad. BH

TABLE OF CONTENTS

ACKNOWLEDGMENTS

Special thanks to Judy Brunner, Dennis Cooper, Carter Cramer, Larry Ewing, Kristie Gallion, Kevin Hurst, Stan Ponder, Ginny Reding, Bob Senninger, Charlotte Spencer, and Debbie Stollenwerk.

INTRODUCTION

As you begin this book, you will find yourself at some specific point on the continuum of finding your first teaching job; or perhaps you will read this as you consider changing teaching positions. This may be the semester you are graduating, and you may be increasingly nervous as you contemplate that you still haven't had an interview. You may also be starting this book as you enter your first semester of professional education classes. Because of the varying points of time and subsequent interest, we have tried to make each of the following chapters function independently, and we have attempted to present the topics chronologically and logically. We hope you will find the material as interesting to read as we found it to research and write.

PART ONE

IN YOUR FIRST YEAR OR TWO OF COLLEGE

*I*f you are reading this book this early, you are one of those people truly blessed by thinking ahead. You must be anticipating teaching or you would not have chosen this book at such an early time in your career. This is a good time to set aside cognition, or your thinking side, and let your affective, or feeling, side take over.

DREAM A LITTLE

*O*ne of us was told to do this exercise by a professor about twenty years ago, and it worked well for us. Dr. George Murphy, who had been at Pennsylvania State University and was my advisor for my master's degree, suggested that I, Genny, get relaxed in a comfortable chair, become quiet, close my eyes, and begin to visualize or think about what I wanted to be doing in five years. I was to take my time and continue to envision until I had a strong positive sense of what I wanted to be doing with my life, with my career, and with myself. Then I was to write about what I had visualized for myself. I cannot remember whether Dr. Murphy stayed with me as I envisioned my future, but I had a strong sense after sitting, considering, and writing of what I wanted to do with my career.

    Whenever students who are not yet certain about what they want to do have approached me, I suggest that they also envision what they want to be doing in five years, as I did. If they wish me to, I will let them discuss with me what they envisioned, but only after they have written down their thoughts. Writing their thoughts allows them to look back later and reflect on their perceptions. Without this permanent record of their perceptions, their thoughts (and yours) may quickly lose shape and evaporate. Writing, either by pen or word processor, tends to promote reflection and contemplation. Those of you who are auditory or kinesthetic in your learning might prefer to audiotape or videotape yourself. Those of you who are visual in your learning might want to use a visual form of brainstorming, such as mapping, webbing, or clustering, which is described in the next section.

9

One particular person stands out in my mind who completed this exercise. Shirey had taught for three years in Florida and was coming back for recertification. She said she had mixed feelings about what she wanted to do with her graduate work. She tried the exercise of closing her eyes and visualizing what she would like to be doing in five years. She found that she saw herself teaching at a community college or junior college. We were in a bit of a quandary because no community colleges were located within a 200 –mile radius of our location. Her visualization, however, gave a focus to her direction of study and the research she pursued in her course work.

By the time Shirey completed her recertification, gained some teaching assistant experience at our university, and finished her master's degree, a community technical college was in the process of being built in our city. Shirey applied for a position with the technical college and was hired immediately to fill it—a particular job in a technical college, neither of which existed when she visualized her dream.

Dr. Murphy, the mentor I have remembered most in all my years of school, also asked his students to write a paper, answering the questions: Who am I? What am I here for? How is my being here worthwhile? Although I think I wrote rather feeble responses to those questions at that time, they have reverberated through my head many times since then, and I have answered better mentally and in writing as the years have passed. I feel I am a better person for having been asked those questions and for finding myself frequently answering them. I hope you will take a few minutes to respond to those three questions now and that you will continue to ask them as the years pass. This activity closely correlates with the section that follows.

MAP YOUR FUTURE

As an alternative or supplement to the dreaming activity explained above, some visual learners may find it helpful to start a dream album. In a dream album, students begin clipping pictures from magazines, newspapers, and other sources. The idea is to locate pictures that capture visually exactly what you want in life, not only in terms of a career, but also a life partner, children, possessions, travel, personality characteristics, advanced education, and other wishes you have for your future. Although neither of us have tried this process, several students have completed this activity and have felt a much stronger sense of their aims and goals and of what is important for them in physical, emotional, intellectual, as well as spiritual ways.

Another similar activity is to use the kind of mapping, webbing, or clustering that we frequently use as educators. Place your name in an oval at the center of a large page of paper, and begin drawing circles outward from that center. In each circle describe with one– or two–word phrases the major factors you are considering in the future. Continue to draw more circles outward from these circles and then add descriptions. Gabrielle Rico, in her book *Writing the Natural Way*, suggests this type of activity, "clustering" in her terminology, to help strengthen writing and free the imagination. She believes that clustering releases the right side of the brain. Those of you who are verbal and visual learners may find this useful in looking at your current and/or future plans concerning career, personal, physical, spiritual, mental, emotional, and other factors. See Figure 1 for an example of future mapping.

Figure 1 – Sample Future Mapping

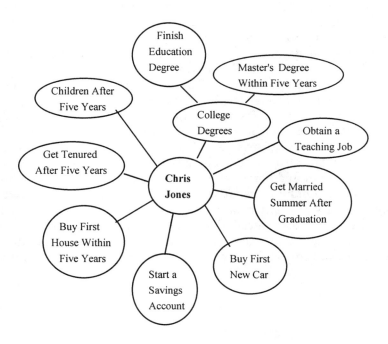

FOLLOW YOUR BLISS

*T*he late Joseph Campbell—anthropologist, mythologist and scholar—urged his readers and those who watched a television series highlighting his work to follow our bliss. He contended that if we choose a life work that brings us extreme happiness and joy, we would live in that joy. In contrast, we could surmise that if we choose a life work solely because the job market is good in that content area and we have probable assurance of tenure, we might be miserable and stifled and feel as though we were living lives of quiet desperation.

While you have time to change your mind, put yourself in as much contact as possible with students at the grade levels you plan to teach and the content material in the subject areas you plan to teach. Many universities now have early field experiences that put you in classrooms earlier. Additionally, you can volunteer or find paying experience that will place you in before–, during–, or after–school experiences to help you test whether you will feel bliss when working with the age levels you are considering. In the next section, specific suggestions will be made concerning finding paid and volunteer positions. Within this chapter, the important point is to find out whether or not you love the subject matter and the students with whom you plan to work. You deserve to find the career that best suits you, and students deserve to have teachers who care about them and are passionate about the subject matter they are teaching.

What is—and is not—bliss? Although it may be dangerous to set standards for someone else, here are some signals about teaching bliss. If you find yourself enthusiastic and passionate as you study your subject matter, that is a definite positive sign. An enthusiastic teacher can involve students. A scholar passionate about his or her area of study can also spread that passion to students. If you find yourself impatient and bored with either students and/or your subject matter, that is a definite negative sign. If you find yourself resentful and cynical as you begin making contact with students and content teaching, consider other grade levels or content that might be more conducive to a fulfilling teaching career. Nothing can substitute for spending actual time working with students and your subject matter.

Hurst and Reding (1999) state in their book *Keeping the Light in Your Eyes* that "when we view school as a place to do what we love with people we enjoy, it becomes more than job" (p. 65).

In spite of the emphasis on enthusiasm and passion stated above, many teachers with quite different personalities and characteristics can find success in teaching. Clarify for yourself as quickly as possible what you believe in and consider essential. A quiet teacher, a humorous teacher, a logical teacher, a scholarly teacher and many others can all reach students effectively and help them learn. Difficulties usually occur when any of these personality types do not respect their students, do not find effective ways to help them learn, or do not stay honest, open-minded, and willing to change or learn. As a teacher becomes unhappy and unfulfilled, it becomes easy for that teacher to blame the students, system, or school. A bitter teacher can unintentionally be responsible for turning one or numerous students, depending on his or her teaching load, against school, learning, and/or a content field. None of us looks in a mirror in the morning and decides to turn against students and blame them for the lack of learning in a classroom. However, none of us also wants to feel personally responsible for negative things happening in a class.

We need to remember that students have little or no choice in the teachers assigned to them in the classroom; whereas, teachers can choose other student age levels, content fields, or professions. The earlier you make contact with students, the quicker you will find out whether or not you are working with the right age level of students, content area, and perhaps even whether you are preparing for the right profession. If you are not feeling joy or bliss in these early experiences, you may be a candidate to be one of the 50 percent of teachers who leave the field within their first five years of teaching.

Teaching is, in our undoubtedly biased opinions, the most important career possible. We are responsible for encouraging joy in learning, for helping shape a collective future. We see it as both an art and a craft. We can start as shaky teachers and become master teachers. Some of us see teaching almost as a calling. Often those with a calling, art, and skill leave teaching for more lucrative or easier fields. We would hope that those individuals who stay in teaching do so not because they are trapped but because they are following their bliss.

PART TWO

PLAN AHEAD DURING YOUR INITIAL
YEAR IN A TEACHER EDUCATION PROGRAM

When first entering your teacher education program, you can plan ahead in several important ways. Although it is sometimes difficult to think so far ahead, it can prove most valuable in the long run if you plan ahead. Even pursuing one of the ideas suggested below can make a big difference in finding a teaching job and particularly finding one closely matched with your interests and talents.

INVESTIGATE

Doing some investigating now can solve some problems for you later. Several things to consider include finding out about your school's placement center, scouting the job market, and learning about teacher standards and tests.

If you are reading this book with a full year to go before you begin to teach, you are in a position to plan ahead to help yourself select a teaching position well–matched to your personality and preferences. Consider the following helpful factors when beginning to plan your future.

Scout the Placement Center

Most colleges and universities have a placement center designed to help students get a job when they get out of college. Now is a good time to pay a visit to your college placement center. Ask your school how their placement center works. Ask about services they have available for teachers; ask about job listings, handouts, or pamphlets that explain how to set up a placement file and about placement timetables and deadlines.

Placement centers also will provide information about teaching area shortages, school districts with job openings, and similar demographic data. Although you would not want to begin

14

preparing in an area you know you dislike, reading about high-demand teaching areas might help you select between areas in which you are equally interested. Placement centers generally have samples of application forms that will help you to know what schools look for, such as professional, organizational, and volunteer activities. To know this can help you consider what activities you may want to elect during your university years.

Assess the Job Market

Assessing the job market now can help you explore possible places to teach or potential majors where there might be teacher shortages. This information can help you narrow your focus if you are undecided about majors, minors, or grade levels.

The placement center will also most likely have a listing of average teaching salaries for different school districts in your area, state, and throughout the county. Be cautious, however, in selecting a major, minor, or grade level on the basis of salaries or need only. A lifetime is a long time to spend working in a content area and with an age level of students with which you are not well–matched. Take advantage of any volunteer or work positions that can help you better gauge the best match for you.

Learn about Teacher Standards

One of the first inquiries you may wish to make is to find out if the university you are attending has state and national accreditation. The National Council for Accreditation of Teacher Education, or NCATE, is usually the accrediting association used at the national level. State–level accreditation is sometimes linked to NCATE but also may have a separate accrediting process. You would benefit from determining whether or not your university is accredited both by the state and NCATE. If your university is not accredited by NCATE and you are considering teaching in a specific state, you may want to inquire about reciprocal certification and whether or not the state in which you hope to teach has a reciprocal agreement with the state in which your university is located. Many states will require that you take some extra courses, even in states with reciprocity.

You may begin to hear about national board certification and want to know more about it. The national board process was started in about 1990, with an intention to recognize only the best of

15

teachers. Teachers who apply complete a complicated process of submitting information, including videotapes of their teaching. Since the process currently costs over $3,000 because of the amount of analysis needed, schools tend to pay for teachers to apply. Only a small percentage of the teachers who apply receive the certification. For schools interested in being recognized as excellent, having a number of teachers with the national board certification is probably the most difficult standard available as yet. This is not a certification to lightly consider applying for until you have several years of teaching experience and a good idea of the high standards required to pass the certification.

Learn about Teacher Tests

*N*ow is also the time to inquire about what teacher tests you may have to take. Many of the required tests have deadlines, and some schools of education require that you take certain tests before being admitted into their teacher education programs or before continuing in the program. Ask questions and set goals for yourself so that you don't let yourself get behind or in a bind. The best place to find out what is required of you is to ask your academic advisor.

You would benefit from learning as much as possible about the tests required at your university and your state. Generally, pamphlets are available that explain the content of most tests. Your advisor should be able to guide you or identify others who can help you. In short, know which tests are required of you.

If you are a student who has trouble with exam anxiety and test–taking skills, check out one or more of the books available in your university library about test–taking skills. Find out if any services on your campus give help with test-taking skills. Two sources are named in the reference list at the end of this book which are particularly helpful in strengthening test-taking skills.

Search the Internet

*T*he Internet has become an invaluable tool for learning more about anything. Do Internet searches on teacher education programs, teacher standards, teachers tests, the job markets in your area and around the country, various salary schedules, professional teaching portfolios, writing resumes, or getting jobs. Just log on and look around various sites. You'll probably learn even more than you knew you had questions about. Also check out your college or university's Web site. (See the end of this book for some useful Internet sources.)

MAKE DECISIONS

*O*nce you have done some initial investigative work and have checked the job market, it is a good time to start making some important decisions that can help you later. Remember that writing allows you to have a permanent record of your thoughts and ideas. If you do some writing about where and whom you want to teach, be sure to date each written record and keep them in a folder where you can refer to them often. Try to keep an open mind about making decisions until you have been able to test your ideas with volunteer work, early field experiences, and other opportunities.

Once you have a fairly clear idea of where you want to teach and whom you want to teach, you can begin planning to reach your goals. The following are some ways to help you obtain a job where you want and with the age level you want when the time comes.

Decide Where and Whom You Want to Teach

*I*n order to decide whom you want to teach, you almost have to work with students in the levels you want to teach. By the time you reach student teaching, it is often difficult to change levels. Therefore, you would benefit from any contact with students early in your program. If your university is one of the many that incorporates early field experiences, try to be placed in a situation as similar as possible to the one in which you tentatively wish to teach. Also look for volunteer and other activities that will put you in contact with students at many age levels. Consider accepting any position at any age level. You may find that you really enjoy working with younger students you assumed you would dislike, middle school students you thought would be intimidating, or high school students you thought would be difficult. To work with students in a school setting or in a similar situation is one of the best tests to help you reach your decision.

Plan Student Teaching and Field Experiences

If you have choices concerning where to student teach or to do field experiences, be sure to request the school where you eventually wish to teach. Remember the old adage "It's not what you know, but whom you know." The reality is that those people hiring teachers are more receptive to people they have seen operating in the classroom so that there are no unpleasant surprises after new faculty are hired. It is not only what you know but also whom you know that helps principals and others to select new faculty over those about whom they know little or nothing. Schools quite often hire people who have previously worked in their schools because they already know them and have seen them work in the classroom.

Consider Minor Areas of Study

As you do a search of job openings, you may notice that a certain subject area is in high demand. If it is an area that interests you, perhaps consider it as a minor. If it is a field related to your own, you might be able to choose it as a minor without having to take too many additional hours. Some courses may count for both your major and your minor. Make these decisions now. A minor could help to make you more marketable in your job search.

As a word of caution, remember that it is unwise to pick up a minor only because that area is in demand. It will be important that you enjoy what you teach as well as whom you are teaching.

TAKE ACTION—GET YOUR FOOT IN THE DOOR

*O*nce you have made some decisions about what you want to do at the end of your college career, you can take specific action to help you reach those goals. You can begin networking with teachers, your fellow students, members of professional organizations, and faculty in the schools where you do your field work. This step can help you "get your foot in the door." You may want to consult Richard Nelson Bolles' book *What Color Is Your Parachute?* Although this resource is not aimed specifically at teachers, it provides helpful advice as you search for teaching jobs.

Two ideas, in particular, are quite useful. First, throughout each annual volume, Bolles makes clear that all job seekers experience problems with self-concept and rejection during any sustained unsuccessful attempts to find a job. The teacher-to-be who is experiencing self-doubt and depression will find profound relief in seeing this phenomenon described in detail. Second, Bolles clarifies the importance of the job-hunter making contact with the individual who does the actual hiring. Bolles then helps the job-hunter develop a game plan that shows him or her the answer to a problem. We encourage you to read either a current or old annual edition, which is often available in libraries and used-book stores. (See the bibliography for further information.)

Network

The dictionary defines *network* as "a group or system of interconnected or cooperating individuals." The purpose of forming these connections with those in education is to help you learn from each other and to have a support system. These groups or individuals can also help you find out about job openings or help connect you to someone who may have a job or know about a job. In all of your dealings with those in education, whether it be your professors, students in your classes, or teachers in your field-based experiences, it is important to make good impressions and to get to know these people. You never know where these connections might lead you. Open doors and never burn your bridges.

Do Volunteer Work

An excellent way to become known by teachers and administration in a school is to do volunteer work. Although you are terrifically busy in school, it is worth undertaking volunteer or paid work in the schools or grade levels that interest you. At one point, two different students talked to one of us. The first was surprised to learn that the middle school students she thought she should avoid were the very students she most enjoyed in her early field experience, and she began to focus on middle school certification. The second graduate student was an experienced sixth-grade teacher who had found, after several years of teaching, that she much preferred working with second graders. Some volunteer work might have revealed this preference years earlier.

Schools are always looking for people to mentor students, help the teachers, or help with things such as lunchroom duty. Some colleges and universities even offer college credit for mentoring through service learning programs. Ask your professors and advisors if they have any such programs at your school, and take advantage of them. As you volunteer in the schools, it will provide you with wonderful hands-on experiences, will help you become known in the schools, and will look great on your resume!

Additionally, volunteer work is a strong way to strengthen your spiritual, or altruistic, side. Many of us find we gain energy and satisfaction from work that puts us in contact with those who need and appreciate help. Since so much of your immediate time is focused on grades and requirements, you may find yourself looking forward to work that is generous and serves others.

Substitute Teach

You may or may not be aware that in many states you can be a substitute teacher even before you earn your teaching degree. This is a perfect way to become known in the schools or districts where you want to teach. Schools often hire their substitute teachers as soon as these teachers complete their degrees because the faculty and administrators have learned the quality of their teaching. Some students plan their class schedules to allow for one or two days a week without classes so they can plan for substitute teaching. They provide the schools with a list of the days they can teach.

If you decide to go this route, take substitute teaching seriously. Keep in mind that you are being observed, even if not formally. Administrators and teachers notice if you arrive on time, if you are dependable, how you dress and behave, or how you handle your students in the hall, at recess, or lunch. The teachers for whom you are substituting care about what you did with their students in their absence. Did you follow their plans? Did you grade papers for the work that you assigned in their absence? Did you leave their room neat, orderly, and perhaps even better than you found it? It matters, and it will definitely be remembered.

Cathy was substitute teaching in a school where she really wanted to teach after she graduated. On one visit, when she was in a class she had been in before and was comfortable, she invited the principal to come in and observe her teaching. The principal was impressed that she felt confident enough to ask him. He observed her teaching, he liked what he saw, and Cathy got a job just as soon as she graduated.

Check with the districts around you and find out how many college hours they require of their substitute teachers. Many school districts are in desperate need for substitute teachers and will probably be thrilled to get you. By substituting, you will also receive a paycheck while you are in school.

Involve Yourself in Professional Organizations

Now is the perfect time to become involved in professional organizations. Most major areas of study have their own organizations, and most of those organizations have a council for students. For example, the National Education Association (NEA) has a student council on the national and state levels, and the Student National Education Association (SNEA) has chapters at most universities. Another example, International Reading Association (IRA), has student councils at most universities. Generally, the cost of joining is much less expensive than it is for teachers, so now is a good time to join and get involved.

Check with your teachers and advisors about the professional organizations at your school and quickly become involved. These memberships can help you form networks within your subject area and can get you started early in your professional development. Be sure to include these activities on your resume, and provide documentation for your activities in your professional teaching portfolio.

Become a Leader

Once you have found organizations to become a part of, let the advisors of those organizations know you are interested in a leadership position. Activities such as these can help set your resume apart from others. Administrators look for people who are leaders actively involved in professional organizations because it shows that these people are lifelong learners who can take leadership positions on committees and school activities.

Additionally, taking leadership roles in student organizations helps to establish the habit of professional involvement and commitment. Leaders in professional organizations find that they have the potential to affect c hange, which can help to counteract helplessness and a victim mentality. Career burnout can sometimes be avoided by working with others to learn new ideas and to receive encouragement and inspiration.

Obtain Part–Time Field–Related Jobs

*A*nother way to get acquainted at the school where you want to teach and to strengthen your resume is to find a part-time job in the field of education. Many schools hire part-time aides. Many schools also have before- and after-school programs for students whose parents work. You might consider tutoring positions either private or with professional learning centers in your area.

The important thing is to build a record of experiences within your field. Do this partly for the addition to your resume, but more essentially to discover whether or not this is the level of students you want to work with for the rest of your career or, at least, at the beginning of your career.

BEGIN YOUR PROFESSIONAL TEACHING PORTFOLIO

*N*ow is the time to begin working on your professional teaching portfolio to present in connection with job interviews. By beginning early, you will know what kinds of documentation to look for during your field-based work in the schools and during student teaching.

By building a professional teaching portfolio, you have the opportunity to visually represent yourself as a teacher. The idea is to show prospective employers what kind of teacher you are. A professional teaching portfolio is a small collection of materials which relates "to one or more dimensions of persons' professional life—their methods, their work, their feelings about their work, and/or their professional growth" which is "selected for a specific purpose" (Olson, 1991, p. 73). The purpose addressed in this book is to use a professional teaching portfolio in order to obtain a teaching position.

Many teachers have obtained teaching positions because of their professional teaching portfolios. One teacher, Dianne, took her portfolio with her on a job interview but wasn't certain what to do with it, so she held it on her lap during the interview. She said the interview was "going okay" but "there weren't any sparks." When Dianne could tell that the principal was about to conclude the interview, she asked him if he would like to see her teaching portfolio. She began showing him several areas of interest in her portfolio, and she said the interview "really started hopping." When the principal called her the next day to come meet the superintendent, he told her to "bring that notebook thing." She got the job.

One advantage of having your professional teaching portfolio is that administrators don't have to try to imagine what kind of teacher they think you'll be; they can see what kind of teacher you are through the evidence of your work.

It is important to note, however, that employers are not only looking at your portfolio, but they are also watching you as you present your portfolio. As you show your portfolio, it is easier to show your excitement about teaching. One superintendent has said that she has applicants bring their portfolios to the interview, although she doesn't really look at them—she is more interested in watching the faces of the teachers as they show their portfolios. Perrone (1991) states that "we look for a sparkle in the prospective teacher's eye" and that "it will be easier to show your enthusiasm as you show your portfolio" (p. 19).

Cole et al. (1991) states that many students see the "portfolio as giving them a competitive edge in the job search" (p. 10). The following story is another example of how a portfolio can give you an edge.

> The Director of Laboratory Experiences at Wright State University received an out-of-state call from a school district personnel director saying that he had interviewed one of our graduates and was moderately impressed. At the end of the interview, the student applicant produced his portfolio. The personnel director looked through it and was greatly impressed by the student's initiative and by the portfolio itself. He offered him the job. (Cole et al., 1991, p. 10)

A professional teaching portfolio has made the difference for many teachers in helping them get their desired teaching positions. A teaching portfolio will help you be on the cutting edge. Portfolios are still new to many school districts, and those who are familiar with them love to see teachers bring them.

23

Decide What to Include in Your Portfolio

A professional teaching portfolio is a good tool to visually represent yourself as a teacher to prospective employers and others. Remember, this is *your* portfolio; the decision regarding what goes into it is solely your own. Barnett (1992) contends that for a portfolio one should select "only those artifacts and reproductions that demonstrate the acquisition of a particular skill, competency or piece of knowledge" (p. 145). Olson (1991) states that "careful and thoughtful selections for inclusion can be guided by asking, *What makes this evidence especially appropriate given the purpose for this portfolio?*" (p. 79). She believes "while portfolio materials may reflect the current status of accomplishments, they might also reflect a person's growth and development" (p. 74).

Hurst, Wilson, and Cramer (1998) state that the contents in a portfolio "should be determined by individual teachers and should vary significantly, depending on each teacher's philosophy, values, and viewpoints as well as on teaching and collegiate experience" (p. 579). A portfolio is a sampling of your work, not a scrapbook. Keep in mind the axiom "less is more." A good size might be a 1/2-inch to 1-inch three-ring binder. Administrators do not have much extra time in the interview process, so a large portfolio might daunt them. The following is merely a *list of suggestions* to give you ideas about the types of things that can go in your own portfolio. You might want to limit the number of sections you include from five to seven.

- *The Cover*. An employer should not have to open your portfolio and flip through it to determine that it is yours. Your name should be clearly readable on the front. You can buy notebooks that have a plastic cover into which you can slide a paper. This allows you to personalize your cover. Many people write "Professional Teaching Portfolio for" and their name on the cover. You can also design your cover to fit your personality or major of study. Covers of portfolios are as varied as the teachers who create them. The cover of a kindergarten teacher's portfolio may differ vastly from the cover of a high school math teacher's portfolio. Make it fit you!

- *Table of Contents*. The inclusion of a table of contents helps the developer better organize the portfolio materials and helps the reader better understand the focus and content of the portfolio. It could note the sections of the portfolio and subsections. Since the portfolio is a work in progress, it is advisable not to include page numbers in the table of contents or on the pages so that the contents may be rearranged.

- *Resume.* Beginning your portfolio with your resume provides a helpful overview of your teaching experiences. The organization and contents can vary considerably among resumes, so teachers should select the particular form which best suits their needs. See the section on resumes in this book for more suggestions.

- *Statement of Philosophy.* A statement of philosophy can provide a written summary of your beliefs concerning teaching. This statement can include the reasons you chose teaching as a career. Although some teachers prefer not to include a statement of philosophy and like to let the portfolio speak for itself, the act of writing a philosophy statement helps you clarify your belief systems related to teaching and can be useful as a learning tool as well as helpful to readers. Zubizarreta (1994) states that philosophy statements need to "put more emphasis on establishing connections between teaching philosophy and actual methods and outcomes by reflecting on the teaching craft" (p. 324). This philosophy could be a section in itself within the portfolio, or it could be incorporated throughout the portfolio by including short statements regarding teaching or learning beliefs in such places as on header pages or above pictures with students.

- *Official Documents.* Official documents can provide needed certification information about teachers. Transcripts, teaching certificates, and ACT, SAT, NTE, and similar documents may be quite helpful in establishing information. You need to be careful in deciding which documents to include. If you wish to emphasize a strong academic background, you would definitely want to include undergraduate and graduate transcripts in your portfolio. A teacher with less than sterling academic grades might prefer to emphasize lesson plans and teaching activities, forgoing including transcripts. Teachers who have received honors and might be reluctant to mention them in interviews, for fear of seeming self-serving, can share that information without a word by including certificates and other documentation within their portfolio.

- *Letters of Recommendation.* Letters of recommendation add strong support for teachers. These letters can be from former teachers, employers, university supervisors, or other professionals. Although the content of letters in portfolios may differ significantly from letters written confidentially for your placement file, letters still give readers a better understanding of you. Professional portfolios provide a good excuse for you to ask former teachers and others to write letters for you. You may want to be cautious about including letters of reference from nonprofessional sources. Although a letter from a clergy member, for instance, might be an asset in one setting, it may be a problem in another setting.

- *Evaluations*. Evaluations provide additional needed support information. Student teaching and aiding evaluations may be the only evaluations available for preservice teachers. Practicing teachers may have additional formative and summative evaluations given by principals or other administrators. Obviously, it is better to omit evaluations that contain negative information.

- *Photographs and Visual Documentation*. Photographs and visual documentation provide among the strongest support items available within your portfolio. The most convincing photographs are those in which you are shown working with groups of students. When working in the classroom, hand the camera to a student, aide, or another teacher and make certain you are frequently included in the photographs. It is important to label or caption pictures to provide a short explanation of why the photo or visual was provided. Include photographs of students, bulletin boards, learning centers, games created, thematic units, and other similar activities.

- *Professional Development*. Professional development is an important aspect of teaching. Your portfolio can show evidence of your growth as a teacher through professional development activities in which you have participated. You can include flyers or programs highlighting workshops you attended, written reflections about those workshops, or evidence of membership or leadership positions in professional organizations.

- **Self–Goals.** Self-goals could be a list of what you want to achieve in your classroom or at your particular school. For example, a goal might be to continue learning and growing by remaining actively involved in professional development organizations. Or you might have a goal of developing a schoolwide reading incentive program such as a read-a-thon.

- **Goals for the Students of Tomorrow.** This section could be a short list of goals you have for your students, such as teaching them how to learn so they will become lifelong learners or teaching them how to become reflective decision-makers.

- **Student and Parent Sentiments.** It is important to include notes and pictures from students and parents. Administrators often find this kind of information invaluable because it provides evidence of the rapport between you and your students and you and your students' parents.

- **Samples of College Work.** Sample, high-quality lesson plans can be included to provide evidence of good planning. It is better to include lesson plans you have actually taught. While including samples of lesson plans written in education classes may be valuable, it is suggested that those with grades or professors' comments on them may not be appropriate to include for appearance's sake. Include a limited number of lesson samples; one or two would be appropriate. One teacher, Debbie, was applying for a special education position for which she was eligible only for temporary certification. When she was called for an interview, the director of special education informed her that there were several strong candidates also applying who were already fully certified. During her interview, she brought out her portfolio and began showing samples of Independent Educational Plans (IEPs) she had written in her graduate classes. The director was so impressed with the quality of her work that she offered her the job. Because of her portfolio, Debbie was offered a position under temporary certification over eight other fully qualified candidates. Actually seeing what Debbie could do outweighed what the director could just imagine the other candidates could do.

- **Thematic Units.** Thematic units are valuable documents to include within portfolios. Since administrators are likely to be quite interested in your ability to plan and carry out instruction, these need to be carefully scrutinized before being included. It is probably better to have one outstanding unit than four poorly organized units. Photographs of student work and displays set up during the thematic unit will provide visual representation of the unit and may do more to sell your abilities than the written unit.

- *Learning Activities.* Include in your portfolio any learning centers or learning activities that have been developed. Explain their usage, if appropriate, and show pictures or samples.

- *Original Ideas.* Include any innovative ideas for positive reinforcement, discipline, bulletin board ideas, lessons, and so on.

- *Examples of Students' Work.* You can include examples of your students' work to show the types of activities you use as a teacher. They can also serve to show students' progress, which reflects positively on teaching ability. Vickie learned from fellow teachers about professional teaching portfolios the day before an important teaching interview. She quickly built her portfolio, in which she included work her students with learning disabilities had done from the beginning of the year through later in the year, which showed the progress they had made. She was offered the job over many other qualified applicants and was told it was because they were able to see through her students' work that she was a dedicated and effective teacher.

- *Personal Data.* Personal data can be included at whatever point you consider it appropriate. If you want prospective employers to be aware of you as a member of a family, you will want to include photographs of you and other family members to give employers a more complete view of you. Some teachers want to separate their careers from their home life and will prefer to omit photographs or other documentation from their personal lives. Some teachers want the personal data section introduced at the beginning of their portfolios to show their families' high priority in their lives; others want the personal data section later to reflect that professional concerns should take precedence; others prefer to omit such sections for professional matters. If you choose to include such data, it is better to keep this information to one page or so in order to prevent detracting from other professional material.

- *Autobiographies*. Autobiographies are sometimes suggested as helpful. Cole et al. (1991) state "many portfolios included autobiographies which helped faculty to know their students better and to see them as multidimensional" (p. 10). Teachers sharing such autobiographies need to keep in mind that the intended audience will be people making hiring decisions, so this particular autobiography needs to omit information which might cause readers to judge the writer negatively.

- *Reflections*. Reflections can be an important addition to a portfolio because they show employers reflective decision-making. You can describe your student teaching experiences, providing insight about what you learned and how you have grown from the experience. In-service teachers can reflect on how they have grown from their years of teaching.

- *Inspirational Items*. You can include poems, sayings, pictures, or articles that have impacted you as a teacher. These may be best incorporated throughout the portfolio.

Snap Photos, Photos, Photos

*I*t is true that one picture is worth a thousand words. When administrators get a visual of image of you in action in your classroom, it leaves a lasting impression that they are not as apt to forget as they might words on a resume. Have someone take photos of you reading to the students, working with groups, or even interacting on the playground. Include photos of field trips, special projects, or student work. Take photos of the activities or displays you are most proud of in your classroom.

PART THREE

THE SEMESTER BEFORE STUDENT TEACHING

*T*he semester before student teaching is the time to get all of your affairs in order because you will be too busy while student teaching. This is the time to set up your placement file, draft your resume, obtain letters of recommendation, and look more seriously for job openings where you want to teach.

WORK WITH THE PLACEMENT CENTER

*A*s mentioned earlier, most schools and universities have placement centers to help their students find jobs upon graduation. They will help you set up placement files and will tell you everything you need to include. Discover the special services your placement center offers. They may have some sample placement folders, resumes, or other models you can see.

SET UP YOUR PLACEMENT FILE

A placement file generally consists of your resume, transcripts, letters of recommendations, and evaluations from field-based work and student teaching. One student, Eric, decided he would not set up a placement file since it is not a requirement. His plan was to send out his own materials. However, the semester during student teaching when he started receiving applications he had requested from schools, he was dismayed to find out that every application he received from over five different states all stated that he needed to have his college send in his placement file. He found himself traveling across the state to his university to try to get his placement file set up at the last minute, which was a very difficult task because he was in school all day, five days a week student teaching. While his friends were signing contracts, he was scrambling to get his placement file in order.

DRAFT YOUR RESUME

One item that is included in a placement file is your resume. Most placement centers will assist students, showing them how to set up a resume. Help can vary from providing samples to offering workshops to providing disks with resume formats. Ask your school placement center how they can help you set up your resume. When you are ready to finalize your resume, you may want to take it to a professional printing service, but if you have a good example to look at, a good computer, printer, and proofreader, you can most likely do as good a job on your own.

Because you still have your student teaching to complete, and because you are still having new teaching experiences, you may not want to finalize your resume at this stage. It will help you immensely, however, if you have it nearly complete so that you can quickly add your newest experiences.

Read about the best ways to put together a resume. Find out what a teaching resume should look like. You can find out by checking out a book from the library, asking the placement center for information, searching the Internet, or checking local printing stores for their professional services. See Figure 2 for an example of a teaching resume.

Figure 2 – Sample Resume

NAME
Street Address
City, State, ZIP
Phone

OBJECTIVE
>Explain type of teaching position you desire.

EDUCATION (List most recent first)
>Year: Degree (For example: B.S. in Education)
>School or University
>Year: High School

TEACHING EXPERIENCE (List most recent first)
>Dates: Substitute teaching
>Name of school
>
>Dates: Student teaching
>Name of school
>
>Dates: Field-based experiences
>Name of school

WORK EXPERIENCE (List most recent first)
>Dates: Employer, job title
>Job responsibilities

EXTRACURRICULAR ACTIVITIES AND ORGANIZATIONS
>List organizations you are involved in
>Highlight leadership positions
>List volunteer work

HONORS AND AWARDS
>List scholarships, grants, invitational honor societies,
>awards, etc.

REFERENCES
>You may write "Available Upon Request," or list names,
>titles, addresses, and phone numbers of references here.

REQUEST LETTERS OF RECOMMENDATION

*I*t is now also the time to ask for letters of recommendation from your professors, teachers in your field-based work, bosses at work, or anyone you feel can represent your work as a teacher well. Administrators and other hiring people recognize general letters of recognition as signs that the recommender does not know you well enough to write much specifically. Professors and other people write letters for many beginning teachers. Make certain the recommender has a visual connection to you so he or she knows which Mary or Mark Jones about whom they are writing. Provide a resume in order to allow the writer to be able to personalize the letter of recommendation. No matter how well you know the person who is writing the recommendation, it is unlikely that he or she can recall perfectly specific information about you.

Most placement centers will have a specific form you are to use for your placement file. Generally, it is a one-page form on which you record your name, major, and social security number. Also, there is usually a section where you are to indicate whether you want a particular recommendation to be confidential or nonconfidential. If you indicate it should be confidential, this means you will never be allowed to see the recommendation. Indicating nonconfidential means you can go to the placement center and read the recommendation any time you wish. While the choice is strictly yours to make, it has often been suggested that letters of recommendation mean more to administrators if they are confidential; it is a mark of confidence. It shows that you are confident that the person whom you asked to recommend you will say good things about you. An indication of nonconfidential may show that you have reservations as to whether you will be highly recommended or not.

When asking people for letters of recommendation, you may ask them if they feel they know you well enough to give you a positive recommendation. This gives the person you are asking a comfortable way out if they feel they cannot give you a good recommendation. Watch their facial expressions and body language as they give you a response to your invitation. If their faces light up and they exclaim they would love to write you a recommendation, then you can probably feel confident that they will write positive things about you. If, however, the person seems to hesitate when you ask or seems to have to think about it, you could respond with, "If you don't feel you know me well enough, I could ask someone else." Since it is wise to avoid neutral or negative recommendations, it is much better to have fewer positive recommendations than more with some bland recommendations.

While asking for letters of recommendation for your placement file, you can also ask if the person would be willing to write a letter for your teaching portfolio. You might have to explain the difference between the two letters as well as their different purposes. The recommendation for your portfolio obviously will be nonconfidential. If the person writing the letter of recommendation is typing it on the computer and running the placement file form through their printer, then it wouldn't be too much more trouble for them to print another copy on school or business letterhead. You may ask different people to write letters for your portfolio than you do for your placement file, but the letters for your placement file are more important.

The people who write the letters of recommendation for your placement file are required to mail it directly to your placement center. You should provide the person with a stamped envelope addressed to the placement center so that they don't have to prepare the envelope and pay for postage.

LOOK FOR JOB OPENINGS

*B*egin checking the placement center now for lists of job openings. You may want to call or write to the schools in which you are interested in applying and request job applications so you will have them on hand when you are ready to apply.

PROFIT FROM COLLEGE TEACHER PLACEMENT DAYS

*B*e sure to check with your advisors and placement center about college teacher placement days. Many graduates find teaching positions at these events. Teacher placement days are events usually sponsored by and held at large universities. School districts from all over the state and surrounding regions are invited to attend. School administrators and personnel are available so that students and schools can learn about each other.

Schools will provide information and many will accept applications and resumes that day. Some districts may go ahead and interview teachers on the spot. Take your professional teaching portfolio with you because even if administrators may not have time to look at it, they are often impressed that you had the initiative to make one. A professional looking cover with your name on it can help keep an image of you in their minds.

Stephanie, an art teacher in her senior year, was hired during her school's teacher placement day even though she still had one remaining semester of student teaching. (She had her portfolio with her!) Because of the school's dire need for an art teacher, they made an unusual agreement with her university to let her be supervised by the university during her first semester of teaching which counted as her student teaching experience. While this does not happen often, what does happen often is that people find teaching jobs at these teacher placement days.

Most schools will let you take a day off from student teaching to attend teacher placement days because they realize how important and effective they are in helping teachers find jobs and in helping schools find teachers. Take part in your school's teacher placement days even before it is time for you to be looking for a job. It will help you get the inside view of how they work, and you can practice asking administrators questions about their schools.

PART FOUR

THE SEMESTER OF STUDENT TEACHING

*T*he semester during student teaching is going to be one of the busiest of your college career. You no longer are just attending classes; you are now in the schools first thing in the morning until later in the afternoon, five days a week. Nights and weekends will be spent writing lesson plans, grading papers, and attending ball games and school events. This is why you completed as much as you could during the previous semester.

Now it is time to wrap up loose ends and complete projects you started last semester, such as deciding to which schools you will apply, completing job applications, polishing your resume, writing cover letters, updating your portfolio, and checking to make sure your placement file is ready to be sent.

MAKE CONNECTIONS WITH WHOM YOU KNOW

*I*f you have had the opportunity to work in the schools where you hope to teach, take advantage of the connections you have made. For example, if you became acquainted with the principal where you want to teach, let him or her know when you are graduating and that you are interested in teaching there. Ask about job openings. Keep your "foot in the door" by staying in contact.

DECIDE WHERE TO APPLY

*Y*ou've been checking the placement center and Internet for job openings, now it's time to make your decisions about where you want to apply. If you have not already called or written to schools to request applications, do it early in the semester.

COMPLETE APPLICATIONS

*T*he appearance of your completed application is essential. As with anything you will be sending to prospective employers, you *must* make absolutely certain that there are no mistakes. Always have someone or several people proofread your work. One error could mean the difference between getting and not getting a job.

Many teaching applications ask you to write your philosophy of education. Do not write your first draft of this directly on your application. Work on it first on the computer where you can edit and change it. Let it set between work sessions so that you are seeing it with fresh eyes. It was once said, "The secret of good writing is rewriting." Take this task seriously. Prospective employers are not only looking to see your philosophy of education; they are also looking to see that you can form sentences correctly to convey coherent thoughts.

POLISH YOUR RESUME

*Y*our resume should be almost ready. All you need to add now are your experiences from this, your last, semester of college. Check to make sure you have included all of your field-based work, job experiences, honors or awards, organizations to which you belong, leadership positions, and your GPA if it is good.

WRITE COVER LETTERS

*W*hen you mail your resume and/or application to the schools where you are applying, also send a cover letter. Your cover letter is the first thing a prospective employer will see of you, so it needs to look perfect. Construct your letter with a great deal of care.

Cover letters are normally only one page on a good quality paper. In your cover letter briefly let the administrator know what type of teaching position you are interested in (your subject area), grade level preference, when you will be available, and any extra duties you would like to be involved in, such as coaching or yearbook sponsor. It is also a good idea to mention in your cover letter that you have a professional teaching portfolio available.

Address the cover letter to a specific person. Generally, you will address the letter to the principal of the school where you are applying. Do not begin your letter with "To Whom it May Concern." Use the name of the person responsible for hiring. See Figure 3 for an example of a cover letter.

Figure 3 – Sample Cover Letter

Your Street Address
City, State, ZIP
Date

Name of Administrator
Job Title such as Principal or Superintendent
Name of School
Street Address
City, State, ZIP

Dear Mr., Ms., or Dr. (Find out and use the correct title):

In this first paragraph state that you are interested in teaching at their school. State your degree, major area of study, when you are graduating or when you will be available. State the specific teaching position for which you are looking.

Refer to your resume and/or letter of application explaining any special qualifications or any unique talents you can offer to the school. You may mention things such as volunteer work or leadership positions in professional organizations.

Your closing paragraph is the place to ask for an interview or a chance to meet with the person. You may also add here that you have a professional teaching portfolio.

Sincerely,

(Sign your name here.)

Your typed name

Enclosures: (Application and/or resume)

Do's and Don'ts of Cover Letters

- DO organize your sentences and paragraphs carefully, looking for spelling and editing errors.

- DO use the spell-check feature of your software on your letter, then proofread the letter carefully as well.

- DO make certain that you have an accurate proofreader edit, if possible, and proofread your letter.

- DO note specific characteristics of the school or town to which you are drawn.

- DO be sure you are writing for a position for which you are qualified or that you have included justification for how you are qualified if it is not apparent.

- DO indicate in your letter if you have particularly appropriate experience or background in relation to the position.

- DO use a good quality paper, such as the same paper you used for your resume.

- DON'T begin the letter with "My name is . . . ." The reader will know whom the letter is from by reading your name on the return address of the envelope and below your signature.

- DON'T brag or exaggerate; it turns administrators off.

- DON'T send form letters to schools; be sure to learn and use the name of each principal or appropriate school official in each letter.

- DON'T permit any spelling or editing errors in your letter.

- DON'T send a one- or two-sentence letter if you wish to be seriously considered.

- DON'T use unusual script or fonts, bolding, or italic for the cover letter. A 12-point readable font is recommended.

- DON'T use paper with a gaudy background or "cutesy" graphics.

Writing Tips

- Use a single central idea in each paragraph, with all sentences relating to that idea.

- Use complete sentences.

- Use various lengths of sentences for variety and smooth flow of words.

- Try to use vocabulary you would normally use; do not consult a thesaurus for unfamiliar or uncommon words.

- Avoid beginning all or most sentences with "I."

- Make certain you use the correct words, such as *there/their/they're* and *too/two/to.*

UPDATE YOUR PORTFOLIO

*Y*our portfolio should be almost ready by this point. Review it to make sure it looks and presents itself in the way you want for interviews. Add pictures, evaluations, cards or letters from students, or anything from your last semester of student teaching that you think is appropriate.

Try to keep your portfolio lean and mean. If you have considered including assignments, make sure they make you look like a knowledgeable professional.

If you cannot decide whether or not to include transcripts, consider the grades you have made. If your grades have not been good, omit the transcripts; do not make it easy for readers to find your weak spots.

FINALIZE YOUR PLACEMENT FILE

A trip or call to the placement center would be appropriate now. Check to be sure everything that is supposed to be in your placement file is included. Have the office check to make certain all of your letters of recommendation have been received and placed in your file. If any are missing, you may have to remind the people you asked to write recommendations for you to send your letters. Consider asking the person reviewing the file to glance at the recommendations to see if there are any that should be removed.

Once you have your applications ready to send to the schools where you applied, give your placement center a list of names and addresses where your file should be sent. You can also call the schools later to make sure they were received.

PART FIVE

JOB INTERVIEWS

You have worked hard to get to this point. Something about your resume or cover letter made you stand out to the employer. You can keep that good impression going with a few tips about the interview process.

BEFORE THE INTERVIEW

What you do before the interview can be just as important as what you do at the interview. Do what you can to learn about the school where you are interviewing, practice answering possible interview questions, and work on one of two questions of your own.

Do Your Homework

Learning about the school where you are going to apply can help you make a good impression. Find out such things as how many students there are in the school or how many classes there are for each grade in elementary school. Is there only one high school math or English teacher? Where will you fit in the scheme of things? Look for a place where you can fulfill a need or a particular niche. For example, if you are pursuing a position as a teacher of students who are gifted and you have learned that the school where you are applying has not had a gifted program before, have a plan or some ideas about how a strong program can be established. You do not want to come on too strong, but you can let the administrator know that you have some basic ideas about setting up a gifted program.

Make sure to know a little bit about the person interviewing you. Is it the principal, superintendent, or a teacher? Find out if he or she has a Ph.D. or Ed.D. and should be addressed as *Dr*. A quick social blunder might be to say *Miss* to a *Dr*. You can find out this information by asking someone connected with the school or by calling and asking the school secretary before the interview.

Anticipate Possible Interview Questions

*P*lan ahead for your interview by anticipating possible questions an administrator might ask and your answers. Ask a friend to help you practice by role-playing. Have your friend ask you questions, to which you respond as you might in the actual interview.

The following is a list of common questions asked in teacher interviews. For more sample questions, see the last section of this book titled Wise Words from Administrators and Master Teachers.

- What is your philosophy of education?

- Why do you want to teach at this particular school?

- What is your discipline plan?

- What are your views about teaching reading? (And don't just expect this if you are an elementary teacher. Because reading is such an important element in learning at all grade levels, administrators from elementary to high school are interested in it.)

- What is your major strength as a teacher?

- What is an area of weakness in your teaching abilities?

Have Your Questions Ready

*O*ften toward the end of the interview the principal will ask if you have any questions. You can let him or her know you are prepared by having a question or two ready. Possible questions might be about what types of extracurricular activities teachers participate in, if the school participates in some form of professional development such as career ladder, or if the school supports teachers to attend professional conferences. The latter will show that you are interested in professional development.

DURING THE INTERVIEW

*T*he interview is your chance to shine. You will want to make a good, strong impression, and you can by following some common sense rules of etiquette and pragmatics, dressing appropriately, seeing the administrators' perspective, and using your portfolio to highlight your strengths.

Put Your Best Foot Forward—Etiquette and Pragmatics

*W*hile you know common rules of etiquette, it might be helpful to have a quick refresher course. Pragmatics has to do with social skills. It has been said that more people lose their jobs because they cannot get along with others than because of job incompetence. Social skills are one of the most important aspects involved in getting along with others—and in getting a teaching job.

Look over the following list, and ask a good friend to *kindly* go over the list with you. Ask if there are any areas that you need to work on.

- When the other person is speaking, really listen; don't be thinking about what you are going to say next.

- Look the other person directly in the eye. Looking around or beyond them can make you look unsure of yourself or dishonest.

- If you are being interviewed by more than one person, look at each person and direct your comments to each of the individuals, not just one person.

- Do not interrupt!

- Be friendly. Smile.

- Do not act like a know-it-all. While you want to give a good impression about your strengths, few things turn people off quicker than someone who brags on themselves or who act self-important.

- Watch the body language and facial expressions of the person interviewing you. You can take cues from them if you watch carefully. For example, if you notice they stop looking at you and

44

start reading their notes while you are still answering a question, perhaps you have answered too long. In this case you might want to quickly end your answer.

- Do not bite your fingernails or lip, play with your hair, or fidget.

- Be careful to be politically correct in your speaking. Use accepted educational terms such as "students with disabilities" rather than "LD kids."

Put Your Best Shoe Forward—Appropriate Dress

*F*irst impressions are lasting impressions, and the first impression is usually based on appearance. If you come to an interview with wrinkles and spots on your clothes, you are apt to make interviewers concerned about how you will look as you teach daily. Make sure you are clean and your clothes are neat. It is best not to wear faddish or outlandish clothes; you are not there to make a fashion statement. The rule for interviews is usually that neither male nor female has bare feet. Sandals, unless worn with hose, are too casual. Jeans and T-shirts are great for almost everything, except a job interview.

Men, nice slacks, a shirt, and tie cannot be beat. Or you could drop the tie and add a sports jacket or wear both the tie and the jacket. Most teachers don't wear three piece suits to school, so you do not need to wear one on an interview—unless you know this particular school would prefer such a look during the interview—but you do need to dress professionally. Be sure your shoes are polished and your clothes are pressed.

Women, a dress with jacket or a skirt and blouse with jacket is acceptable. Do not wear short skirts, frills, or tight-fitting dresses. Have a sense of the school before you choose to wear a pantsuit. Avoid party dresses or evening wear that would be clothing you would never wear to school. Avoid being too casual in your dress; you will want to dress professionally like a teacher. Interviewers assume that you will wear your most appropriate teaching clothing to the interview; try not to disappoint them.

Women, watch your accessories and grooming. Long dangle earrings and large hoops are more risky than smaller earrings. If you use nail polish, be careful that your nails aren't chipped and that you have no dirt under your nails.

If you feel all of this is too restrictive to you as an individual, by all means, dress to suit yourself. Don't be too surprised, however,

45

if you are not given the position. Interviewers are trying to hire professionals proud of their teaching. Unless they know you or your credentials are outstanding, they may be afraid that this is the best they will ever see of you and may be understandably hesitant to hire someone who is risky even at the interview.

Put Your Best Words Forward—Standard Language Usage

*B*y the time of the interview, it may be too late to start working on your proper use of language. However, many jobs, teaching and otherwise, are lost because of the use of poor grammar without the interviewees' understanding. People who use nonstandard grammar are often not aware of their misusage. After a few minutes of an interview, people conscious of language usage will be building a case against particular candidates. Since so little is available in an interview by which to evaluate candidates, grammar and sentence usage can frequently eliminate a candidate from consideration.

If you have reason to believe you may have a problem in this area, work to help this area. For instance, speak to a friend, professor, or family member with whom you are in frequent speaking contact. Ask that person to pull an ear, rub a nose, or use some other signal when you have made a mistake. Notice and ask them about the problem. You may want to wear a golf watch or some other tally instrument in order to keep track of the number of mistakes you make in a day.

Check at the library or in your college's writing center for some resources that note the most frequent kinds of mistakes. Several sources are listed in the reference section of this book. Write down those you have trouble with and fit them into the conversation until you feel you have learned to use them.

An awareness of some common oral grammar problems might be helpful. Some students have difficulty with noun-verb agreement such as the following: Using *I, you*, or *we* with *done*, as in "I done the work" instead of "I did the work." Using *hisself* instead of *himself* is also a common problem. Saying *between you and I* instead of *between you and me* will be bothersome to some interviewers. The application of *me and John* instead of *John and I* could also hurt your chances of getting a job. Remember—always put the other person first. A commonly mispronounced word is *especially*, often said *exspecially*. If you are called for an interview and the principal asks to speak to you, answer by saying, "This is she (or he)," not "This is her (or him)."

46

Understand Administrators' Perspectives

As with any situation when dealing with people, it is always good to try to see the other person's perspective. Realize the administrator is also in a somewhat stressful situation. He or she has the awesome responsibility of finding and hiring the best teacher available who will best fill the vacancy at the school. Getting rid of teachers once they are hired is an unpleasant and sometimes difficult task, so administrators are under pressure to find just the right teacher. They spend hours poring over resumes and letters, they make dozens of reference calls, and face the frustration of "telephone tag." Then they interview many candidates, asking the same questions repeatedly.

By trying to understand the administrator's situation as well, it might help put you at ease somewhat and remind you to be pleasant, enjoyable, and easy to work with during the process.

Expect Committee Interviews

A trend at many schools these days is for prospective teachers to be interviewed by interview committees. The committee is generally made up of a group of teachers and an administrator. Being interviewed by a committee of people can be intimidating. During interviews by a group, remember to make eye contact with everyone in the group. Teachers will notice if you seem only to address your questions or answers to the administrator. Give the respect to the teachers as you would an administrator.

One of the characteristics the teachers in the group might be looking for is collegiality. They want to know how well you can get along with others. It is important that you be yourself. Be friendly and easy to talk with. Try to be at ease as much as you can.

The types of questions you will be asked by the teachers are the same types of questions administrators will ask.

Expect Videotaped Interviews

Some schools use videotaped interviews so that they may go back and review the interview. If you know you will be applying to a district where they use videotaped interviews, you can be more prepared if you first practice by videotaping yourself. Get a friend to help you. You can set up a video camera at your kitchen table. Have your friend ask you possible interview questions. Stop and watch the tape. Did you fidget or play with your hair? Watch those idiosyncrasies and then practice again. Each time, watch yourself on tape and then try it again until you feel confident in your "performance."

If you don't have access to a video camera, check with the media section of your school's library. Some schools have cameras you can check out and others have rooms designated for you to use in the library.

Present Your Portfolio

*T*he professional teaching portfolio helps provide a self-portrait of you as a teacher. In the interview process your portfolio will be a visual aid as you discuss aspects of yourself as a teacher. Think of it in terms of a chart or a handout that a presenter would use when making a speech; it is only a tool. Consider what Perrone (1991) said about the employer looking for "your enthusiasm as you show your portfolio" (p. 19).

On an interview Anne held on to her portfolio because she did not know what to do with it. When the administrator asked her a question about discipline, she responded by saying, "Would you like for me to tell you, or would you prefer that I show you?" In her portfolio she had a copy of a discipline plan she had written in one of her college classes. The principal asked a question about her views on communicating with parents, and she showed him a sample of the newsletter she developed for her class during student teaching. It is one thing to say, "I developed a newsletter for parents," but entirely more effective to show one you have made. The principal was extremely impressed, and she got the job!

Instead of handing your portfolio to the interviewer when you begin an interview, most teachers prefer to hold it and then use it as the need arises. Remember the story about Dianne; it was nearly the end of the interview when she asked the principal if he would like to see her portfolio. Be prepared that the administrator may not want to see your portfolio; some administrators would rather adhere to their own structure of interviewing. Do not push your portfolio on anyone.

Also, let your portfolio speak for itself. The portfolio allows you to show what you can do and what you have accomplished. Be cautious not to undo all the good of your portfolio by bragging about your accomplishments. Do not say things such as "This shows what a good teacher I am." Instead say something like "This is an example of how I teach." To someone who has read numerous application letters and has listened to many candidates, a "red flag" goes up when an interviewee exaggerates his or her ability to teach. Some committees eliminate candidates who write or say something like "You will never find a candidate as well qualified as I am." Overstatement might be effective in some fields, but teachers and administrators tend to be suspicious of those who sing their own praises too much, particularly while criticizing other professionals.

Another way to present your portfolio is to offer to leave it after the interview. This gives the administrator time to look through it at his or her own pace and provides you the opportunity for a second face-to-face interaction the next day.

Some principals have stated that they do not have time to look through the portfolio carefully. Yet, they are still impressed with applicants who have them because it shows the applicants have initiative and organizational skills and are dedicated professionals.

AFTER THE INTERVIEW

After the interview, always send a thank-you letter or card to the lead interviewer or administrator thanking him or her for the interview. You may express your appreciation for being interviewed or say that you were impressed with the school. You might even say that you are even more interested now in teaching at the school after seeing its positive environment. If you met teachers, you might mention their names and say that you enjoyed meeting them.

PART SIX

THE CONTRACT DECISION

*R*eceiving your first teaching job offer is perhaps one of the most exciting times of your life. Savor it and celebrate it!

DECIDE IF THE JOB IS RIGHT FOR YOU

*W*hile interviewers were interviewing you, you were also interviewing them. If you discovered that the philosophy of the school is one you will be unable to live with, you may want to consider this fact strongly before accepting a position at this school.

One effective way of considering whether or not to teach at a particular school is to make a list of pros and cons of working at the school. In the left column, list reasons why you want to accept the position; in the right column, list reasons why you do not want to accept the position. It does not really matter which list is longer. The important factor is what you feel after completing the lists.

Any hesitation will probably depend on several factors. If you interviewed seven months before the start of fall term, you are likely to be more hesitant than if you interviewed three weeks before the start. If you are considering moving hundreds of miles away, you will probably hesitate more than if you live close to the position. If you are in a high-demand field with many openings, you will probably be more hesitant than if you are in a low-demand field with few openings. If you strongly disliked the principal, the superintendent, or the teachers you met, you are likely to be more hesitant than if you liked them. Your list of pros and cons will help you to weigh all of these and other related factors.

If you learn better by talking through a situation, you may need to find a willing ear to listen so that you can sort through your doubts and questions. Ask your friend to just listen without intervening. If you have no one who can just listen, check with the counseling center at your university. Counselors are trained to listen while you talk, allowing you to work through your situation.

50

SELECT AMONG MULTIPLE OFFERS

If any of you have received more than one job offer at the same time, you are fortunate indeed, but may be in something of a quandary. You may be in this situation if you are in a high-demand field and/or have outstanding credentials.

In this situation, you are likely to be rushed by both sets of interviewers to make a decision. You may be told, "We need to know by tomorrow whether or not you can take the job." Rehearse ahead of time your response, depending on what is happening. For instance, it is perfectly legitimate to say: "I've scheduled an interview in two days with another school. I will need two days after that to decide." Schools that rush too much are often those that find themselves second best in too many instances. Unless you know solidly that the second school will be inferior, ask courteously to be allowed to go through the second and/or third interview.

Again, the list of pros and cons can be useful. Then finally, follow your instincts. As Dr. Benjamin Spock used to tell the parents of his patients, you know more than you think you do.

MAKE THE DEAL

If you are in a position to negotiate, this is the time to ask for whatever you consider essential. This is the time to negotiate your salary and benefits, such as insurance, sick days, or retirement benefits. It is appropriate to ask how the district handles pay adjustments, such as cost of living increases or pay raises for further education. You might ask to see the school's salary schedule.

If you are being asked to take on the cheerleader sponsor's or assistant coach's position, be sure that you communicate at this time any agreements you want in writing. Some schools pay you for extra duties and some do not; find out now what this school does for extracurricular duties. Be sure you know whether you are getting a salary for nine or twelve months. Also be sure you understand what other activities are part of your position; you do want to know what you are getting yourself into with the position. Be careful, though, not to seem so reluctant to do the work expected that the offer might be withdrawn.

Know where your teaching room is and whether you or your students are likely to be moving. Do you have a desk? What supplies are available? These questions may be asked of a fellow teacher or school secretary if you are reluctant to talk with the interviewers about them.

Sign only one contract at a time. Most school boards will release you from a contract. However, some will penalize you if you break a contract after a certain date and you may have to pay them to break the contract.

PART SEVEN

WISE WORDS FROM ADMINISTRATORS
AND MASTER TEACHERS

*F*or this section, principals, superintendents, and teachers were asked to write about what they look for in teacher candidates. Among them they hire dozens of teachers each year. Consider their words carefully.

PRINCIPAL, JUDY BRUNNER

*"T*here will be times in your educational career when you will truly believe that classes, homework, student loans, practice, and final examinations will be all there ever is in your busy, hectic life. However, before you know it, you'll wake up one morning and discover that you're no longer an undergraduate, and the world of employment is before you. Trust me—it's a great feeling, but your first thought may be to crawl back into bed and pull the covers over your head.

Just how do you get a job? What will make you the right choice? There are no simple answers, but Judy Brunner feels there are a few things to consider as you begin the application and hiring process.

- Take time to neatly and thoughtfully fill out the teaching application.

- Dress appropriately for the interview. Clothing should be neat and businesslike. (This is not the time to show off those new, wild earrings.)

- Take several copies of your resume to the interview.

- Be prepared to be interviewed by a committee. This can be intimidating, but it is the committee's responsibility to put you at ease.

- Be prepared—at the end of the interview you may be asked if you have any questions. Questions regarding salary, faculty morale, extracurricular sponsorships, or professional development would be considered appropriate.

- Know some things about the school in advance. Show that you have "done your homework" and have taken the time to research the school community.

- Take your portfolio to the interview, if you have one.

- Do not drink caffeine or eat chocolate before the interview if you are subject to panic attacks and extreme nervousness. Before going into the interview room, take several deep breaths and exhale slowly. Close your eyes and start counting backwards from 100. By the time you get to 75, you will feel better.

- Do not tell the interviewers that you feel nervous. Speak slowly and with confidence. Make eye contact with everyone, not just the principal.

- Ask the committee if you fully answered a question if it seems particularly complex or your answer rather lengthy. It will show a sincere desire on your part to be thorough and honest.

- Be prepared that some type of interview evaluation form may be used; many school districts have them. You may be rated on communication skills, personal appearance, self-confidence, emotional maturity, sensitivity, creativity, and enthusiasm.

- Do not answer questions too quickly. Even if you have a ready response, you might want to say, "That's a good question. May I have a minute to think about it?" Pause then give your answer.

Brunner also suggests that you have a friend ask you some of the following sample questions before an interview. Practicing answers aloud can be extremely beneficial.

- What are your professional experiences?

- What principles will you use to motivate students?

- What is the most exciting thing happening today in your area of study?

- Describe the physical appearance of your classroom.

- If a visitor walked into your classroom during instruction, what would he or she see?

- How will you provide for a wide range of students' abilities in your classes?

- Could a nonreader successfully complete your class?

- How would students describe you?

- What is the role of homework?

- How will you communicate student progress to parents?

- How would you handle a student who has a consistent behavioral problem in your class?

- How will you contribute to the development of the total school program?

- In a school setting, what does the word *flexible* mean to you?

- How would you handle a disgruntled parent?

"Higher education has taught you a great deal, but you've still got a lot to learn. May you never lose that spark, anticipation, and excitement that comes from learning something new that will make you a better teacher and person. We all need renewal.

"Happy job hunting!"

PRINCIPAL, BOB SENNINGER

"As an elementary principal, a wide variety of application letters and resumes cross my desk. Every year I interview a number of people as well. The following information includes some techniques I believe to be important in the entire process of being hired as a teacher.

"It is important for any prospective teacher to project a professional image, beginning with the resume and cover letter. Your resume should be one to two pages in length, emphasizing your educational strengths. Experiences such as student teaching, substituting, practice, and the like are the types of things that are likely to be of interest to a prospective employer. For your cover letter, stationery with educational imagery printed on its borders is very nice, but not the best for a first impression. Use a good quality bond paper, perhaps one with a subtle texture. Keep the letter brief, highlighting your specific objective and why *you* are the one for the job. A final tip here is to PROOFREAD before you send anything."

Senninger advises that you dress professionally for the interview. The size and location of the district does not matter; it is vital that you look sharp.

The next impression you will make is with your verbal interactions. Remember to focus on what you say and how you say it. Confidence is a must, but overconfidence is a problem. Poor grammar will trigger a "Don't call me; I'll call you" response in a hurry. Demonstrate high energy and be positive during the interview. However, be sure to be the same person after you are hired.

At the interview be prepared to ask some good educational questions; for example, "Are the curriculum guides designed in such a way so the teachers can use them easily for lesson preparation?" DO NOT ask what the pay will be! You will find out soon enough if the district has serious intentions about hiring you. Information regarding pay, benefits, time off, etc., are things you need to know at the time you have to make a permanent decision. Before you leave the interview, ask what the hiring timeline will be for your position. If you are given the opportunity to speak with teachers in the building, ask some sound educational questions that will elicit responses reflecting the overall climate of the school.

Always follow up your interview with a formal letter of thanks, once again promoting your qualifications and talents and why they should hire you for the position. Write this letter as soon as you return home from the interview. Because you should already know the employer's timeline for filling the position, call your interviewer a few days before the deadline to express your interest in the position and to check your status.

Senninger adds, "Be clear and concise with your intentions. Do your 'homework.' Acquire a basic knowledge of the school districts you are applying to, and know to whom you need to direct your inquiries."

SUPERINTENDENT, DENNIS COOPER

*"F*or the past twenty years I have been responsible for hiring school personnel—teachers, administrators, and support staff. While we hear much said lately about a teaching shortage, it is still a very competitive market. The good jobs will go to those who have most prepared themselves for the job market.

"Every component of the job search is important and should be approached with the utmost preparation. However, I want to focus on one component that I feel is critical to your success in landing the job—REFERENCES. This preparation begins with the first teacher education class in which you enroll.

"When you begin taking classes in teacher education you will begin developing a network of potential references. This will culminate with your cooperating teachers in your student teaching experience. All of the professors, supervisors, cooperating teachers, school administrators, and anyone you come in contact with during field-based experiences are potential references. It is critical to your success that you demonstrate to these individuals that you have a sincere desire to teach. It is also important to demonstrate a competence that will lead to a successful career as an educator.

"Your application will ask you to provide a list of references. Some application forms will allow as few as three references. It is important that you can provide names of individuals who are considered to be credible. When I call in reference to a teaching candidate, one of the greatest influences on my decision comes from my trust in the person providing information about the candidate. I may even call someone I know in the teacher education department or at the school where you did your student teaching even if that person was not included in your list of references."

Cooper concludes, "Your references or personal contacts may be the key you need to land the ever important interview."

SUPERINTENDENT, LARRY EWING

*"T*he Rolla School District No. 31 enjoys an excellent reputation and features three schools that attained the coveted Blue Ribbon Schools award. Our system enjoys this reputation and has garnered awards and recognition, thanks to the dedicated staff that we employ. We understand that recruiting and selecting teachers is one of the most important things that we do. Each year we introduce new faculty

into our system, and it is paramount that these be the best teachers available. Accordingly, our school district utilizes a very rigorous application process.

"Our certification personnel application is rather long, and we require a great deal of information from the applicant. A candidate demonstrates her or his interest in our school system by completing and submitting all components of the application file. We require the following items for an applicant's file to be considered complete: (1) completed application form, (2) complete set of college transcripts, (3) placement file (preferred) or three letters of recommendation, (4) copy of Missouri teaching certificate or letter(s) verifying eligibility for such, and (5) completed criminal records and child abuse-neglect background check. The application form and file are active for one year but may be renewed or updated in person or in writing. Without renewal, the file will be retained as an inactive file for two years and then it will be purged.

"In our opinion," Ewing continues, "the most important section of the application is entitled 'Professional Statements.' In this section the applicant is asked to respond to seven questions in her or his own handwriting. These questions are intended to reveal the applicant's education values and philosophy. Our assistant superintendent in charge of personnel and instruction scores the responses. The applicant's score on these questions is recorded. This score determines whether or not the applicant will be scheduled for an interview.

"The initial interview is videotaped. The applicant is asked to respond to 22 questions. These same questions are asked of all certification applicants. Again, these questions are intended to assist us in determining whether the applicant shares the education values and philosophy stressed by our institution. The videotaped responses are also scored and recorded.

"We prefer the videotaped interview process for several reasons. One, it can be conducted at any time during the year. We have developed a library of these videotapes for future reference. Two, the applicant's videotape may be watched by several members of our district's leadership team at different times. In other words, a building administrator may at her or his leisure check out one or more of these videotapes to watch. Three, when we anticipate a vacancy, the administrator(s) may go to the videotape library and assess any or all of the applicants by using the videos on file. Four, this structured videotaped interview reduces the interjection of the interviewer's prejudices and the opportunity for the applicant to control or take over the interview process.

"Those applicants who score well on the videotaped interview may be invited back to interview with one or more building administrators and teachers. This traditional interview process affords the applicant the opportunity to ask questions about a specific school campus or program. It also affords the administrator and opportunity to ask specific questions relevant to a particular teaching assignment.

"Is this process more labor-intensive? Yes. Does it require a good deal more from our applicant than the traditional interview process? Yes, definitely it does require more. Does it result in our knowing more about the applicant and how well she or he might fit into our system? Yes, we firmly believe that it does. We have had applicants tell us that it was the most complex process they had been through. We take that observation as a compliment and an indicator that we are right on track. Our process promotes uniformity, at least in the first two phases. By the time the applicant reaches the personal interview phase, she or he should realize that we are very interested in her or him as a professional.

"With the exception of school buildings, a teacher is our system's greatest investment. By that I mean that over the course of a teacher's career, should she or he spend most of it in our system we will have invested a great deal of money for salary and benefits and a great deal of time in orienting and developing that professional. It is therefore incumbent upon us to choose well. We believe today's graduates are better prepared to enter the profession. Recent graduates are coming to us with a better understanding of learning styles, the infusion of technology into the instructional process, and serving as a facilitator of learning. We believe our system benefits from the infusion of newly trained professionals into our established faculty. Again, we simply want to do all that we may to select those new professionals wisely," states Ewing.

TEACHER, KRISTIE GALLION

*"H*aving served on many teacher interview committees, I can say the key to getting a teaching job is professionalism. In every aspect, an applicant needs to appear, speak, and convey thoughts professionally. At the interview, in the pictures in your portfolio, and in other contacts, applicants should dress appropriately for the situation. Although classroom dress has become less formal over the years, a too-casual appearance at an interview can leave a poor impression. Watch your speech habits when interviewing. And, lastly, in

interviews, which may include situational questions, always speak carefully, ensuring the confidentiality of former students."

TEACHER, GINNY REDING

"Several years ago I was asked to speak to a class of education majors at a university in the city where I live. One of the things I was to discuss with them was the importance of preparedness and professionalism in their job searches. I have often been asked to have a student teacher in my middle school English classes. Something I had noticed through the years was that more times than not, the information sent to me from prospective student teachers was full of errors. Students were extremely careless in their writing. This disturbed me a great deal, and I wondered if the same was true in the applications our school receives for job vacancies.

"I asked our superintendent if I could go through the files to see the applications which had come in for new positions during the previous year. What I discovered was quite interesting. The files had been divided so that those who were not even considered for jobs were filed together behind the ones that were going to be considered. All of the files in the back, without exception, had some sort of mechanical or usage error on the application or cover letter. The applications in the front of the files were most often error-free. I made transparencies of some of these applications (with names deleted, of course) to show at my presentation, hoping students would recognize the importance of careful editing and proofreading of their work, especially if it is something as important as a job application."

INTERNET RESOURCES

- http://teach.virginia.edu/curry/class/edlf/589_004.
  Click on "Students' Electronic Teaching Portfolios."
  Electronic portfolios

- http://www.asd.com
  American School Directory. School information about 106,000
  K-12 schools.

- http://www.edweek.org/htbin/fastweb?searchform+view2
  Job listings.

- http://www.microsoft.com/homeessentials/articles/resume/resume.
  asp
  Job hunting ideas and suggestions, resume information.

- http://www.washingtonpost.com/parachute
  Based on 1998 edition of book *What Color is Your Parachute?*
  Information about jobs, resumes, contracts, research.

- http://www.stetson.edu
  Information about job-hunting, resumes, cover letters.

- http://www.iloveteaching.com/Interview/Index.htm
  Interview tips, possible questions, situational questions

- http://www.damngood.com/jobseekers/tip.html
  Resume information and samples. Fifty job-seeker questions.

- http://www.geocites.com/~newteach/finding.html
  Job search resources, professional teaching portfolios
  information.

- http://www.ets.org.praxis
  Information about the Praxis Series.

- http://www.ets.org.praxis/prxstate.html
  State-by-state requirements for the Praxis Series.

REFERENCES AND FURTHER READINGS

Banis, W. J. 1998. The art of writing job-search letters. *Planning Job Choices: 1999 Four-Year College Edition*. National Association of Colleges and Employers, 55 –61.

Barker, J., and Kellen, J. 1998. *Career education: A developmental approach*. Upper Saddle River, NJ: Merrill/Prentice Hall.

Barnett, B. G. 1992. Using alternative assessment measures in educational leadership preparation programs: Educational platforms and portfolios. *Journal of Personnel Evaluation in Education*, 6, 141 –151.

Bolles, R. N. 1998. *The 1999 what color is your parachute?: A practical manual for job-hunters and career-changers*. Berkeley, CA: Ten Speed Press.

Bolles, R. N. 1998. *What color is your parachute workbook*. Berkeley, CA: Ten Speed Press.

Bugliani, A. 1992. The MLA interview: What candidates should know. *ADFL Bulletin*, 24:1, 38 –39.

Campbell, D. M. 1996. *How to develop a professional portfolio: A manual for teachers*. Needham Heights, MA: Allyn & Bacon.

Cole, D. J., Lasley, T., Ryan, C. W., Swonigan, H., Tillman, B., and Uphoff, J. 1991. Developing reflection in educational course work via the professional portfolio. *GATEways to Teacher Education*, 4:1, 1 –12.

Cook, D., and Kessler, J. August, 1993. The professional teaching portfolio: A useful tool for an effective job search. *ASCUS Annual*, p. 15.

Cowden, R. L. 1990. Interviewing successfully—The right moves. *Music Educators Journal*, 77:2, 37 –39.

Coxford, L. M. 1997. *Resume writing made easy: A practical guide to resume preparation and job search.* Scottsdale, AZ: Holcomb Hathaway.

Criscito, P. 1996. *Designing the perfect resume: A unique "idea" book filled with hundreds of sample resumes created using WordPerfect software.* Hauppauge, NY: Barron's Educational Series Inc.

——. 1997. *Resumes in cyberspace: Your complete guide to a computerized job search.* Hauppauge, NY: Barron's Educational Series Inc.

De Vries, M. A. 1991. *The complete word book: The practical guide to anything and everything you need to know about words and how to use them.* Upper Saddle River, NJ: Prentice Hall.

Farrell, C. S. 1993. Black coaches convention focuses on job-hunting strategies. *Black Issues in Higher Education,* 14:9, 25 –27.

Fry, R. W. 1996. *"Ace" any test.* Franklin Lakes, NJ: The Career Press Inc.

Gilbert, S. D. 1998. *How to do your best on tests.* New York: Beech Tree Books.

Gonyea, J. C. 1996. *Electronic resumes: A complete guide to putting your resumes on-line.* New York: The McGraw-Hill Companies, Inc.

Herbster, D. L. et al. 1991. *A flawless method for first-year teacher employment.* (ED329545).

Hurst, B., Wilson, C., and Cramer, G. 1998. Professional teaching portfolios: Tools for reflection, growth, and advancement. *Phi Delta Kappan,* 79(8), 578 –582.

Hurst, B., and Reding, G. 1999. *Keeping the light in your eyes: A guide to helping teachers discover, remember, relive, and rediscover the joy of teaching.* Scottsdale, AZ: Holcomb Hathaway.

Hurst, D. M. 1988. How to obtain international employment in ESL –K-12. (ED299796).

Jandt, F. E. 1996. *Using the Internet and the World Wide Web in your job search*. Indianapolis, IN: JIST Works Inc.

Karl, S., and Karl, A. 1997. *How to get your dream job using the Web*. Scottsdale, AZ: The Coriolis Group.

Lorenzen, E. A. 1996. Career planning and job searching in the information age. (ED399385).

McBride, J. 1998. Job-search strategies to begin the next millennium: Strategies and tools for marketing yourself to employers. *Planning Job Choices: 1999 Four-Year College Edition*. National Association of Colleges and Employers, 14 –18.

Meyers, J. N. 1997. *The secrets of taking any test*. New York: LearningExpress LLC.

National Art Education Association. 1985. Finding a job in elementary and secondary education. (ED302477).

Olson, M. W. 1991. Portfolios: Education tools. *Reading Psychology: An International Quarterly*, 12, 73 –80.

Paris, S. G., Lawton, T. A., Turner, J. C., and Roth, J. R. 1991. A developmental perspective on standardized achievement testing. *Educational Researcher*, 20:5, 12 –20.

Partnership for Academic and Career Education. 1996. Seeking employment in the 90's: Job search guide. (ED408452).

Pawlas, G. E. 1995. The structured interview: Three dozen questions to ask prospective teachers. *NASSP Bulletin*, 79:567, 62 –65.

Perrone, V. 1991. *A letter to teachers: Reflections on schooling and the art of teaching*. San Francisco, CA: Jossey-Bass, Inc., Publishers.

Rico, G. 1983. *Writing the natural way*. New York: Jeremy P. Tarcher.

Shertzer, M. D. 1996. *The elements of grammar*. New York: Macmillan Publishing.

Strunk, W., and White, E. B. 1995. *Elements of style*. Needham Heights, MA: Allyn & Bacon.

Thompson, D. S. 1993. Getting hired: Strategies for job searching that work! A resource guide for early childhood and elementary education majors. (ED360274).

Tierney, R. J., Carter, M. A., Desai, L. E. 1991. *Portfolio assessment in the reading-writing classroom*. Norwood, MA: Christopher-Gordon Publishers, Inc.

Valencia, S. W., Hiebert, E. H., and Afflerbach, P. P., eds. 1994. *Authentic reading assessment: Practices and possibilities*. Newark, DE: International Reading Association.

Zubizarreta, J. December, 1994. Teaching portfolios and the beginning teacher. *Phi Delta Kappan*, p. 324.

INDEX